Crazy for Horses

Karen Briggs
and
Shawn Hamilton

Scholastic Inc.

*To every kid who is as horse-crazy as I am,
and to Pokey, the most generous teacher I've ever had.*
—Karen Briggs

*To Nicola, Christopher, Morgan, Connor and Riley.
A special thanks to all of the generous horse owners and riders
that this project allowed me to meet.*
— Shawn Hamilton

Scholastic Inc.
555 Broadway, New York, NY 10012, USA

Scholastic Canada Ltd.
175 Hillmount Road, Markham, Ontario, Canada L6C 1Z7

Scholastic Australia Pty Limited
PO Box 579, Gosford, NSW 2250, Australia

Scholastic New Zealand Limited
Private Bag 94407, Greenmount, Auckland, New Zealand

Scholastic Publications Ltd.
Villiers House, Clarendon Avenue, Leamington Spa, Warwickshire CV32 5PR, UK

First U.S. printing October 1999

ISBN 0-590-52136-5

6 5 4 3 2 1   Printed in Canada   9/9 0 1 2 3 4/0

The Oldest Breed on Earth

It's hard to imagine that, of the hundreds of different breeds of horses we have today, all trace back to a single wild type, but it's true. The horse didn't always have the familiar look we now know, either. Imagine him as a little swamp-dwelling creature, about the size of a border collie, with five toes on each foot! That was the first ancestor of the horse, *Hyracotherium* (sometimes called *Eohippus*, the dawn horse), who lived some 50 million years ago.

The horse has one of the most complete fossil records, so scientists have been able to trace horses' development over the millennia, as they gradually got larger and switched from living in marshy areas to the open plains. Because they needed to run on hard ground rather than tiptoe through squishy footing, they also lost most of their toes, until they were standing on a specially adapted middle toenail called a hoof. It took millions of years, but eventually little *Hyracotherium* became mighty *Equus*, the modern horse.

That wild ancestor of the modern horse is still with us, in the form of the Przewalski's Horse (pronounced serve-OW-ski). Przewalski's Horse first showed up during the last Ice Age. He has survived in remote areas of Asia to this day. At one time he was thought to be extinct, but Russian explorer Colonel Przewalski discovered a herd running free in an isolated part of Mongolia in the mid-1800s. Unfortunately, human hunters have made the Przewalski's Horse extinct in the wild, but zoos around the world are actively breeding this prehistoric horse, and some are now starting programs to re-introduce them to their natural habitat.

At first glance Przewalski's Horse looks more like a mule than a horse. He is small and stocky, averaging about 13 hands (52 inches), and he is always a yellow dun color with what's called a dorsal stripe down his spine, and zebra striping on his legs. His brushy mane stands straight up and is shed completely every year. He has no forelock, and his tail looks like a donkey's, with a switch of hair just at the bottom. He has a rather large head for his body size (some would call him ugly) and he is definitely wild — very suspicious of humans, and likely to attack you if you come too close!

But despite his appearance, most experts agree that he is indeed the ancestor of all modern horses, from the elegant Arabian to the enormous Shire. When humans first tamed the horse, it was likely an animal that looked very much like the Przewalski's Horse of today. It is selective breeding, over the centuries, that has given us all the wonderful types of horses we now know.

Handy Horse Facts

Pony or horse? How do you tell which one it is? The dividing line is usually a height of 14:2 hands (14 hands 2 inches) at the withers. (One hand is 10 centimeters, or 4 inches.) If an animal is 14:2 hands or under, he is officially a pony. If he's even half an inch taller he's officially a horse. But in some breeds the rule is ignored. The Icelandic, for example, is always called a horse despite being pony-sized, because he is descended from larger horses. And ponies like the Irish Connemara are always called ponies even though changes in their care and environment over the years have caused them to grow larger, sometimes up to 15 hands.

Breeders distinguish ponies from horses by their looks as well. Ponies have some traits — such as a shorter, rounder body, a shorter head, tiny ears and cuter looks — which are called "pony character." Ponies are usually longer-lived than horses, often surviving into their 40s (20 to 30 years is the usual lifespan of a horse). Many people also consider ponies smarter than horses. That's why riding a pony can be quite an education!

GAITS: the ways in which a horse moves. Humans have two gaits, walking and running; horses usually have four – the walk, the trot or jog, the canter or lope, and the gallop. Some horses (such as the Paso Fino, the Saddlebred and the Tennessee Walking Horse) have special ways of moving their feet, to provide a smooth ride for their owners; these horses are called "gaited."

HAND: a unit of measurement for a horse's height; one hand equals ten centimeters or four inches. Horses are measured from the ground to the top of the withers.

POINTS: a horse's mane, tail, muzzle, tips of the ears, and the lower legs – a bay horse, for example, has black points, while a chestnut one has points the same color as his body.

SOUND: description of a horse with no health problems or lameness.

STUD: a farm where horses are bred; also a slang term for a stallion.

TACK: equipment, usually made of leather, used to ride or drive a horse; can include saddles, bridles and harness.

Facing page: Welsh pony

Andalusian

Which horse has a history tracing back to the Roman Empire, and today performs in movies, in the bullfighting rings of Spain and in dressage arenas around the world? It's the noble Andalusian, the "Pure Spanish Horse" which originated in Spain's southern province of Andalusia.

The Andalusian is descended from native Spanish horses and ancient Iberian and Barb horses from the East, who came to Spain with the Moors in the seventh century A.D. The Andalusian was the favored mount of royalty throughout the Middle Ages — it is believed that Richard the Lionheart rode an Andalusian during the Crusades.

History tells us about the human casualties of war, but it seldom speaks of the terrible loss of equine lives — and the Andalusian's dependability in battle almost became his undoing. These noble horses were used in battle whenever Spain was at war. Thousands were killed on battlefields over the centuries, thousands more were stolen by enemy armies, and at one point the breed almost became extinct. But beginning in the late 1400s, at three isolated monasteries in Terez, Seville and Cazallo, Carthusian monks established studs for the Andalusian, keeping the breed's blood pure for generations. Now, no longer threatened by war, the Andalusian has begun to thrive again, both in Spain and in neighboring Portugal, where he is called the Lusitano.

The Andalusian excels at dressage, the ultimate ballet between horse and rider. He is capable of the most difficult and advanced dressage movements, such as the *courbette*, *capriole*, *piaffe* and *passage*. Many ancient prints and paintings of princes and nobles on horseback, performing these maneuvers, feature Andalusians, their regal Roman profiles and long flowing manes and tails unmistakable.

The Andalusian was also a major influence on the Lipizzanner, the "dancing white horse of Vienna," as well as other European breeds such as the Holsteiner and Hanoverian.

Most Andalusians are gray, though some bays, blacks and roans do show up occasionally. They are compact in build, usually standing about 15:2 hands, and have dramatically arched necks and massive chests. Though they can be fiery in temperament, they are fast learners and very dramatic to watch. This makes them a favorite of circus performers and historical filmmakers, as well as dressage enthusiasts.

Fast Fact

Andalusians are thought to have been among the horses brought to the New World by the Spanish Conquistadors, and may be one of the ancestors of the modern-day mustang. Zorro's magnificent black mount in the film *The Mask of Zorro* is an Andalusian.

Appaloosa

The heritage of the Appaloosa is as colorful and unique as its eye-catching coat patterns. Spotted or "raindrop" horses have been appreciated by humans throughout history. Ancient cave drawings, dating back 20 000 years in what is now France, depict horses with Appaloosa spots, and so do images in ancient Chinese art. Among the horses the Spanish introduced to North America in the 1500s there must have been some with raindrop spots, because eventually these horses made their way into the lives of Native North Americans. The Nez Percé tribe that lived in the northwestern United States took a particular liking to the spotted horses. By the early 1700s they had a large herd, and were one of the only tribes to breed selectively for specific traits, especially intelligence, speed and that colorful coat.

White settlers, who started moving into Nez Percé lands around 1860, first named the spotted horse a Palouse after the nearby Palouse River. Over time, the word was slurred to Appalousey and finally to Appaloosa.

In 1877 the U.S. government ordered the army to remove the Nez Percé from their lands so that settlers could take over. Appaloosa horses helped the Nez Percé, led by the famous Chief Joseph, evade capture on an 1100-mile ride over rugged, punishing terrain. When the Nez Percé were finally defeated, their horses were taken from them.

In 1938 a group of dedicated people formed an organization to try to bring the breed back. They found an Appaloosa stallion owned by a Nez Percé man who had quietly been breeding horses for years, and more spotted horses were found running wild in mustang herds. In a few years over 5000 spotted horses had been found.

Today the Appaloosa is especially popular with those who compete in Western events. He is a superb ranch and trail horse, and versatile enough to compete in many other events. In honor of his heritage, he is often shown in native costume classes, which are beautiful to watch. The Appaloosa's good horse sense and patience also make him a great horse for children.

The different coat patterns in the Appaloosa breed range from a white blanket on the rump (sometimes decorated with spots), to large dark leopard spots on a white background, to many tiny spots called snowflake, frosted or marble roan. Registered Appaloosas must also display some other characteristics unique to their breed: striped hooves, a mottled muzzle and an eye that looks like a human's, with white showing around the dark pupil. Many Appaloosas also have a sparse mane and tail.

Fast Fact

The coat pattern of a mature Appaloosa cannot always be predicted when he is born. Many foals are born solid-colored, and "color out" later in life.

Arabian

Of all the horses in the world, there is no other breed so beautiful, so pure or so ancient as the Arabian. He truly seems to be a fantasy from a tale of the Arabian Nights, with his classically dished face, the muzzle that could fit into a teacup, the large and expressive eyes, elegant tapering ears, and nostrils that flare wide to "drink the wind."

The exact origins of the Arabian horse are lost in the shifting sands of time, but we know that he has inhabited the desert for over 4000 years. The Bedouin people who tamed him believed their horses were a gift from the gods, and told many romantic tales about their beloved animals. One legend tells how Allah fashioned the south wind into a creature who "shall fly without wings."

The Bedouins considered their Arabians not only transportation, but prized members of their families, and often welcomed their horses to sleep in their tents at night. Mares were the favored mounts of the Bedouin warriors, as they were thought to be the wisest and most courageous.

The Bedouin tribes bred Arabians for extraordinary stamina and toughness, so that they could survive the harsh conditions of the desert. Their horses could travel for great distances without food or drink. Even today, no other breed rivals the Arabian in long-distance competitive trail riding.

When Europeans wanted to improve the quality of their riding horses, they imported Arabians to cross with their native mares. Arabians contributed elegance, speed, intelligence and soundness — their legs and feet were sturdy without looking coarse. Today almost every single light-horse breed (horses used for riding versus heavy work) has been influenced by the Arabian. The Thoroughbred, in particular, owes many of its best qualities to the influence of three Arabian sires.

In addition to his beautiful face, the Arabian can be identified by his gracefully arched neck, his short back and the way he carries his tail high, like a flag. He is usually small, ranging between 14 and 15:2 hands, and he comes in gray, bay, chestnut, roan and, rarely, solid black (which is much prized).

Regardless of the color of his coat, the Arabian always has black skin, which helps keep him from getting sunburned in the desert. He has unusual intelligence and a sensitive nature, but with good handling he can be a wonderful family horse, versatile enough to participate in many different disciplines and be as loyal a friend as he was to the Bedouins.

Fast Fact

A rare but extremely prized marking of some Arabians is called "bloody shoulders" — a pattern of darker, reddish hairs on the neck and shoulders of a horse who is otherwise gray. Legend has it that this marking commemorates a courageous Arabian mare who carried her injured master a great distance to bring him back to his family after he was wounded in battle.

The Canadian

The first horses to gallop on Canadian soil were unloaded in Quebec City in 1647. They had come from the court of King Louis XIV in France, and were of Arabian, Andalusian and Norman bloodlines, and only half had survived the long sea voyage. Between 1647 and 1670 a total of 40 horses made the trip to the New World. From then on, France sent no more since its resources had been exhausted by all the wars in which it was involved. The original group of 40 horses flourished and reproduced for the next 150 years.

Life in Lower Canada (as French Canada was called then) was hard. The winters were bitterly cold, and the settlers in the colony required the horses to work long hours to help clear the land for farming. Sometimes food was so scarce that the horses were forced to eat the bark from trees to survive. The difficult conditions eventually stunted the horses, making their offspring smaller but hardier. Today the Canadian horse remains one of the toughest, most rugged breeds in the world, and has been nicknamed "the little iron horse."

By 1850 there were over 150 000 Canadian horses in what is now Quebec and Ontario. But so many horses were exported to be used by armies in the American Civil War, the Boer War in South Africa, and for working sugar plantations in the West Indies, that the breed was in danger of disappearing. The introduction of mechanized farm machinery also threatened the existence of the Canadian horse, for he suddenly wasn't needed for general farm work. By the 1960s there were fewer than 400 purebred Canadian horses in existence.

In the 1970s efforts began to bring the Canadian horse back from the brink of extinction. With only eight distinct bloodlines left from the original breeding stock, it has been a challenge — but today Canadians number about 2500, and they are slowly growing in popularity.

The Canadian is an "all-purpose" horse, useful both for farm work such as plowing, and for pulling a carriage or carrying a rider. He has also been the choice of several of Canada's top international driving competitors. The Canadian horse is long-lived and robust, with round, hard hooves that rarely need shoes. His kind nature and willingness to please make him a wonderful family horse. He stands between 14 and 16 hands, and is usually black, although there are occasional bays, chestnuts or dark brown horses. His long, thick mane and tail are one of his trademarks.

Fast Fact

Many people have noted that the conformation (basic overall build) of the Canadian and the Morgan are very similar. Some believe, in fact, that Figure, the founding stallion of the Morgan breed, was the foal of Canadian parents. Since Quebec (where the Canadian originates) and New England (the home of the Morgan) are geographically close, many historians agree there may be some truth to the story that Canadian blood runs in Morgan veins.

Hanoverian

Which breed of horse won five gold, one silver and two bronze medals at the 1996 Olympics? It was the elegant and powerful Hanoverian, bred for generations to excel at the sports of show jumping and dressage. The results at the 1996 Games were no fluke, either — Hanoverians also won a total of thirteen medals at the 1992 Olympics in Barcelona, proving they are some of the world's best sport horses.

The Hanoverian originated in northern Germany, in the former kingdom of Hannover (now the state of Lower Saxony). A flourishing horse-breeding industry, focused on producing robust cavalry horses, has existed there for over 400 years. A State Stud was established at Celle in 1735, and the bloodlines of most modern Hanoverians can be traced right back to this time through the extensive records kept by the government over the centuries.

The Hanoverian is known as a warmblood — a horse which combines the best qualities of hot-blooded horses (Thoroughbreds and Arabians) and cold-blooded horses (draft breeds such as the Belgian or Shire). Throughout the Hanoverian's history, breeders have occasionally introduced bloodlines from other breeds to improve the quality of the offspring, a process which continues today.

After World War II the focus of the Hanoverian breeding program changed from producing horses for the military to breeding the ultimate athletic riding horse for competition. To make sure that the quality of the Hanoverian stays high, the German government tests young horses before they are approved for breeding. Both mares and stallions undergo performance testing which challenges their jumping and dressage ability as well as their willingness to learn. The way the horses move at the walk, trot and canter, and the quality of their temperaments, are also examined. Only the very best mares and stallions are approved to produce foals.

This attention to quality has resulted in tall (usually between 16 and 17:3 hands), noble-looking horses with a lovely, elastic way of moving, a cooperative temperament, and outstanding ability for the highest levels of competition. Hanoverians are much in demand internationally, and are now bred around the world, always adhering to the strict standards set by the German *verband* or breed association.

Fast Fact

One of America's most successful dressage horses, Graf George, is a Hanoverian. The big gray gelding represented the U.S. Equestrian Team many times in international competition. With Guenter Seidel in the saddle he helped the U.S. to win a bronze medal in dressage at the 1996 Atlanta Olympics.

Icelandic

Out on the isolated, windswept, volcanic island of Iceland, hundreds of miles from everywhere else in the north Atlantic ocean, live the descendants of the horses the Vikings rode when they first settled the island in 981 A.D. Not only is the Icelandic breed ancient, it's also one of the purest in the world — because no other horses have been imported to Iceland for over a thousand years.

The Vikings knew how important horses were to their survival in Iceland, and horses were revered in Viking mythology. The most famous mythological horse was Sleipnir, a magical pacing horse with eight legs.

When a Viking warrior died in battle, he would often be buried alongside his best mount. Today horses remain an important part of Icelandic culture, and there are an estimated 80 000 on the island — a huge number considering the human population of 270 000.

The harsh environment of Iceland has produced an extremely hardy little horse, usually pony-sized (between 13 and 14:2 hands) but still referred to as a horse. Icelandics have dense coats and long, shaggy manes and tails to protect them from the cold, and can survive on very little feed. Iceland's environment — volcanic eruptions, rock slides, quicksand and rivers with changing currents, plus a bitterly long and cold winter — can be dangerous. Only the smartest and bravest horses survived, and to this day Icelandic horses have a reputation for not being "spooky" in frightening situations. They are also extremely sure-footed and strong, and despite their small size have no trouble carrying large adults.

But the most remarkable thing about the Icelandic horse is the number of ways in which he can move his feet. In addition to performing the normal gaits of walk, trot and canter, Icelandic horses also pace (move the two legs on one side forward at the same time, like a Standardbred pacer) and perform a uniquely Icelandic gait called the *tölt*, which is extremely comfortable for the rider.

Icelandic laws continue to keep the breed pure even today — once an Icelandic horse leaves the island, he is not allowed to return. Exporting horses to other countries is now one of Iceland's biggest businesses, as Icelandics — lovable, easy to keep and lots of fun — are in huge demand both in North America and Europe. There are now over 100 000 Icelandic horses living outside their native country.

Fast Fact

An Icelandic performing at the *tölt* can keep up with most other horses at the gallop!

Morgan

In 1789 in Springfield, Massachusetts, a mild-mannered schoolteacher named Justin Morgan was given a yearling colt called Figure in partial payment for a debt. The little bay's background was something of a mystery, but he promised to be a nice light riding horse, with his straight, clean legs, his strong, deeply-muscled hindquarters, his little fox ears and big, expressive eyes. Nonetheless, Figure was so small that Justin Morgan was unable to find a buyer for him, so he took the horse home to Vermont.

Over the next 30 years, the little stallion (who matured to be only 14 hands tall) became a local legend. He worked long hard hours in the fields without complaint, he pulled tree stumps better than the big draft horses, he traveled great distances with his master on his back, and he won races against horses nearly twice his size. Justin Morgan's friends and neighbors began to speak with admiration of "the Justin Morgan horse," and they sent their mares to be bred by him. As a breeding stallion, Figure really shone — for regardless of the kind of mare he bred, the foal was a carbon copy of his sire. His remarkable ability to "stamp" his offspring soon made him the single founder of the Morgan breed, the first all-American breed of horse.

Versatility is the Morgan's trademark even today. He's the ideal family horse, equally clever and appealing when ridden with either English or Western tack, or in harness. Not only are Morgans hard workers and easy keepers, staying round and plump on very little feed, but they're also hardy, long-lived, gentle and flashy-looking, with high knee and hock action.

The present-day Morgan differs little from his famous ancestor — he's small but mighty (averaging 14 to 15:2 hands), and tends to be bay, brown or chestnut, though occasionally a buckskin, palomino, black or gray Morgan appears. He's stocky in build, with a short back, powerful hindquarters, deep barrel and a neck set high on his shoulders. And when he flashes past with his head high, his eyes bright and his nostrils wide, he's unmistakably a Morgan, no matter what tack he's wearing.

Fast Fact

Morgans are the oldest purely American breed of horse. They have been an important influence on many other American breeds, including the Saddlebred, Standardbred, Tennessee Walking Horse and Quarter Horse.

Paint and Pinto

If you're looking for a horse who'll truly stand out in a crowd, think COLOR — as in the splashy, flashy spots of a registered Paint horse.

On the Western plains of North America, two-tone horses have long been a favorite of Native Americans and cowboys alike. The history of *pintado* horses (the Spanish word for painted) has been woven into Western songs, stories and artwork. When Native warriors could not find a coveted spotted horse, they would paint their plain horses with special symbols in an attempt to create the Paint's magical beauty. In many tribes Paints were the most treasured horses in the herd.

Though the wild, wild west has been settled for many decades, a colorful part of our Western heritage lives on in the Paint horse. Today's Paint has the distinctive stock type conformation that made him so useful for ranch work — he's compact, heavily muscled, sturdy and able to turn quickly and explode to top speed from a standing start. Many Paints, in fact, are full-blooded Quarter Horses —but a regulation against "excessive white" that the American Quarter Horse Association put in place in 1940 meant that these two-tone horses could not be registered. The American Paint Horse Association was formed to give these animals a place to get registration papers, and to encourage breeders to produce stock horses with the extra eye-appeal of spots. A registered Paint must now come from parents who are registered Quarter Horses, Thoroughbreds or Paints. A spotted horse who is not from this sort of background is called a Pinto, and a separate breed registry exists for him.

Whether Paint or Pinto, spotted horses come in two basic patterns, called *tobiano* (tow-bee-YAH-no) and *overo* (oh-VAIR-oh). *Tobianos* have large, regular spots which are often oval or round, four white legs, a dark face (often with a marking such as a star or a blaze), and a two-tone tail. *Overos* have spots which are irregular and scattered, bold white head markings, and often have dark legs and a tail of one solid color. The white markings on an *overo* do not cross the back of the horse between the withers and the tail. Some spotted horses have characteristics of both coat patterns; they are called *toveros*.

Fast Fact

Though spotted horses are often thought of as being Western, splashy spots are becoming increasingly popular in the English disciplines too. Pintos, such as the Dutch Warmblood stallion Art Deco and his offspring, are making a mark in the show ring — so watch out for spots in the show jumping, eventing and dressage arenas.

Paso Fino and Peruvian Paso

Want a ride so smooth that you can carry a glass of water on horseback and never spill a drop? Do you like a horse who's naturally gentle and friendly, but has a little bit of Spanish flair? Then you'll fall in love with a naturally gaited Paso Fino horse.

The Paso Fino has been bred in Latin America since the Conquistadors invaded in the 1500s. He is a mixture of three fine European breeds — the Andalusian, the Spanish Barb and the now extinct Spanish Jennet — who first arrived in Santo Domingo (now called the Dominican Republic) with Columbus's second voyage to the New World. Other voyages would add to their numbers in Mexico and South America, and they soon came to be known as *Los Caballos de Paso Fino*, the horses with the fine step.

Fancy footwork is the Paso Fino's claim to fame. He walks and gallops just like most other horses, but instead of doing a bone-jarring trot, he does a special gait all his own. His feet fall in the same sequence as in the walk, but are totally even in cadence, so a rider on board barely moves. When it's done slowly, with restrained energy, it's called a Classic *Fino*. Pick up the pace a little, and it's called a *Paso Corto*, the best ground-covering, trail-riding gait. With maximum speed and extension it's a *Paso Largo*.

Though Paso Finos are small (between 13:2 and 15:2 hands, with the average being about 14 hands), they are dramatic to watch, with a special energy and fire that the Spanish call *brio*. They come in every equine color, including palomino, buckskin and pinto. Paso Finos are popular both for children and for older people who don't want to be bumped around by a trotting horse. Because the ride they give is so smooth, they're also an ideal choice for riders who have arthritis or have suffered an injury — and their sensible dispositions make them a popular choice for trail-riding.

The Peruvian Paso horse, a cousin to the Paso Fino, originated in Peru from the same original stock. Slightly larger than the Paso Fino, the Peruvian Paso is also known for its *termino* —a graceful, rolling, outward motion of the foreleg which makes him look like a human swimmer. But his talent for the Spanish gaits makes him just as much a "Cadillac ride" as the Paso Fino.

Fast Fact

In the show ring, Paso Finos are sometimes ridden over a *fino* board, a large piece of plywood laid flat on the ground. As the horse moves over the board, the judge will listen for the rhythm and regularity of the footfalls as his hoofs tap on the wood. The best Paso Finos are as regular as a metronome.

Quarter Horse

More people own a Quarter Horse than any other breed of horse in the world. The Quarter Horse developed from the tough, stocky Chickasaw horse, which in turn was a descendant of the Spanish horses that were first brought to the New World in the 1500s. Colonists crossed the smaller Chickasaw horse with taller Thoroughbreds, and the result was a useful little horse who could do a bit of everything.

One of the early American settlers' favorite sports was getting together for a friendly horse race. The races were usually held on country lanes or roads, which were often about a quarter of a mile long (about 400 meters). The best racehorses were the ones who could explode forward into a gallop from a standing start, and sprint to top speed in just a few seconds. They soon became known as Celebrated American Quarter Mile Running Horses, which was eventually shortened to Quarter Horse. The Thoroughbred might have been faster over a long distance — but for the short sprint he was left in the dust by the muscular Quarter Horse.

By the early 1800s the demand for a rugged and willing horse to help conquer the newly explored American West gave the Quarter Horse a new job. Hitched to covered wagons, or saddled for long-distance riding, Quarter Horses brought the settlers past the Mississippi River into the Western frontier. And they soon demonstrated another talent — a quality called cow sense, the ability to almost read the mind of a cow and figure out where and when she will go. Ranchers with large herds of cattle found Quarter Horses valuable work partners when it came to rounding up the herd or moving it from place to place. Not only were they smart and powerful, they were sensible too, putting in a long day's work without complaining, and rarely becoming nervous the way some higher-strung horses would.

Infusions of Thoroughbred blood made the Quarter Horse a little taller and less stocky, but he retained the basic characteristics which make him unique: a face with a broad forehead and a large, flat jaw; sharp little ears; powerful shoulders and hindquarters; a short back; and a broad, deep chest. At 14:2 to 15:3 hands, he is a handy size for nearly everybody. His heavy muscling makes him very good at sports that require sprinting speed, such as barrel racing and polo, and he can turn on a dime, which makes him wonderful for working cattle. But one of his best qualities is his laid-back personality, which makes him a wonderful first horse for a child or adult.

Fast Fact

Quarter Horses come in a wide variety of colors, including palomino, buckskin, bay, brown, black, roan, *grulla (GREW-ya)*, gray and chestnut, but a whopping one-third of all registered Quarter Horses are sorrel, a blond chestnut color.

American Saddlebred

With fire in his eye, ribbons fluttering in his mane, and flashy feet snapping up under his chin with every stride, an American Saddlebred in action is the spectacular peacock of the horse world. But his origins were humble.

Back in the 1600s colonists coming to North America brought with them Galloway and Hobby horses — small, hardy animals who performed a single-foot gait that was very comfortable to ride. Through selective breeding the colonists developed a horse called the Narrangasett Pacer (reputed to have been the kind of horse Paul Revere rode on his famous ride to warn that the British were coming). Horses that paced or gaited rather than trotted were much valued for their smooth movement in an age when many people spent long, hard hours in the saddle.

In 1706 the first Thoroughbreds were imported to the American colonies and crossed with the Narrangasett Pacers to produce a larger horse which retained the ability to gait. Crosses of Standardbred, Morgan, Arabian and Hackney (a high-stepping English carriage horse) were also added. Over the years, these horses became prized by plantation owners in Kentucky, Missouri and Tennessee, men who needed a horse that could take them all over their large properties in comfort. Because the plantation owners also wanted something flashy which would bring admiring glances from their neighbors, they bred their horses for high knee and hock action and an elegant high-headed look. In the 1800s the breed began to be known as the American Saddle Horse, or Saddlebred.

All Saddlebreds can walk, trot and canter, but some (called five-gaited horses) can also perform the other two gaits the breed is famous for: the rack and the slow gait. Both gaits have the same arrangement of footfalls — the rack is just the fast version, and it can be thrilling to watch, while remaining very comfortable for the rider.

A Saddlebred show horse's naturally high hoof action is enhanced, during training, by adding heavy pads and weights to his hoofs, so that when he walks without them he lifts his hoofs high. His tail is often surgically altered so that it arches up over his hindquarters. In the past, cruel methods were sometimes used to encourage horses to look spirited and pick their legs up higher, but regulations now prohibit these practices.

Saddlebreds are also good at jumping and dressage. They range from 15 to 17 hands, come in all colors (including pinto and palomino), and have beautifully arched necks (called swan necks) set high into very sloping shoulders. Their croups are quite flat, and they have long sloping pasterns to help provide the springiness necessary for a comfortable ride.

Fast Fact

During the American Civil War many famous generals rode American Saddlebreds into battle, for these horses had excellent stamina and were so showy their presence was an inspiration to the troops.

Shetland Pony and Miniature Horse

Who's that peeking out from under the thick, shaggy forelock, with the cheeky look in his eyes? It must be a Shetland pony, the smallest of all the pony breeds.

Shetland ponies originated on the Shetland Islands off the northern coast of Scotland — a harsh, barren place with bitter winds and little food or shelter. No one is sure how they got there. Some say they were brought by the Vikings who settled the island over a thousand years ago. What is certain is that the unwelcoming environment meant only the cleverest and toughest ponies survived. To conserve body heat, each generation got a little smaller, with short legs, a thick neck and tiny ears. The ponies also grew a heavy winter coat and thick mane and tail.

The Shetland Islanders used the ponies to bring peat from the bogs for fuel, and seaweed from the shore to fertilize the fields; they even wove their fishing nets from the ponies' tail hair. Though Shetland ponies are extremely strong for their size, they were rarely ridden — but today they are much in demand as riding ponies for children. At under 11 hands, they are the perfect size for young children learning to ride — even if their extreme intelligence and naughty sense of humor sometimes make them a challenge even for adults!

If you like Shetlands you'll also be charmed by the Miniature Horse, the smallest horse breed in the world. Though he is pony-sized, the Miniature is really the product of a careful breeding program using small horses, and he should have the proportions of a shrunk-down horse, rather than the stocky plumpness of a Shetland. Minis are truly tiny creatures, and are too small (no more than 33 1/2 inches high at the withers) to be ridden by anyone but a small child . . . but that doesn't mean they are just pasture ornaments. Many Mini enthusiasts show their horses in-hand (like showing a dog on a leash), and Minis are also capable of pulling a carriage. They need all the care of a full-sized horse, but they are inexpensive to feed and keep, cuddly and affectionate. Some have even been housebroken and live indoors.

Fast Fact

When the Mines Act of 1847 banned children from working in mines throughout Great Britain, many Shetland ponies were drafted into service in their place. They could travel into the narrow underground shafts to carry out loads of coal. Pit ponies often spent years working underground, rarely — if ever — seeing the light of day. Though they were usually well cared for, it was a harsh life. In a few mines in Britain, Shetland ponies continued in service right up until the 1970s.

Shire

The largest of all the breeds of horses are the draft breeds — horses bred for pulling heavy loads. And the largest of all of the draft breeds is a gentle giant called the Shire.

Despite his enormous size (averaging 16:3 to 19 hands), weight (1500–2000 pounds), and strength (he can pull over two tons of weight in a load), the Shire is a kind and hard-working soul.

It is believed that Shires are descendants of the Old English Black Horse, or simply Great Horse, the huge beasts who were ridden into battle by medieval knights hundreds of years ago. Because the knights wore armor weighing up to 400 pounds, they needed an immensely powerful yet docile horse to carry them.

In the 1700s and 1800s the Shire's job description changed, and he became very popular for farm work and for pulling heavy wagons. The coming of the Industrial Revolution in England put him even more in demand, as huge loads of materials needed to be shipped to and from the new factories.

The invention of the internal combustion engine threatened the Shire with extinction at the turn of the century, and by the late 1940s there were almost no registered Shires in all of North America. But fortunately this gentle breed is now making a big comeback. Though they are still considered rare, there are now over 1000 Shires in North America.

The Shire is almost always black, gray, brown or bay, with lots of white markings on the face and four white stockings on his legs. He also sports what are called feathers — a heavy fringe of hair on the lower legs, which originally helped to protect his legs from the mud when he was used for plowing or pulling a wagon. Now the feathers help show off his snappy action at the trot, when he flexes and lifts his knees and hocks with vigor.

Today Shires are much in demand as show horses, hitched singly or in large groups to wagons and carriages. But when you look at a Shire's long, noble head, it's not hard to imagine him clothed in gleaming armor, gallantly carrying a brave knight into battle.

Fast Fact

Shires are often crossed with Thoroughbreds to produce a horse with the size, sturdiness and easygoing temperament of the Shire and the speed, refinement and stamina of the Thoroughbred. Such horses are much in demand for sports like fox hunting, and are sometimes called heavy hunters.

Standardbred

In 1849 in Orange County, New York, an ugly bay colt named Hambletonian was born. No one suspected at the time that he would be the founder of both a new breed and a brand new sport.

Hambletonian had a special talent. He was the fastest trotter the United States had ever seen, and he passed his speed on to his sons and daughters. Soon the racing that the local farmers did for fun when they met on the back roads near town became big business — and today Hambletonian's descendants race at night, under the spotlights, showing off their blistering speed when hitched to tiny, lightweight sulkies or "race bikes."

The name Standardbred arose because, in the early days, any horse who could trot a mile at a certain standard of speed qualified for registration. Standardbreds now race at either the trot (a two-beat gait in which diagonal legs move forward at the same time), or at the pace (also a two-beat gait, but the legs on one side of the horse move forward at the same time). Most Standardbreds can do both gaits, but the ability to go really fast in one or the other runs in families, so the son of a pacing mare will usually turn out to be a pacer himself.

Closely related to the Thoroughbred, the Standardbred has many of the same streamlined characteristics, but tends to be a little smaller (averaging 15:2 hands) and has a longer body, for more power in harness. His head is sometimes a little coarse, yet full of intelligence. In fact, Standardbreds tend to be calmer than their galloping racehorse cousins. They're quick learners and are good-natured — in short, they're real "people horses." Bay and brown are the colors which predominate, though they can also be chestnut, black, gray or roan.

Though he's a harness-racing specialist, that's not all the Standardbred can do. In some countries he is raced under saddle — and Standardbreds who have retired from racing are now becoming increasingly popular as show and pleasure horses for families. Religious communities like the Amish and Mennonites, who don't believe in driving cars, prefer well-trained Standardbreds to pull their buggies. And the new sport of combined driving (a rugged triathlon for horse and carriage) has provided a new arena for him to show off his many talents.

Fast Fact

Though it's rare to see a speed record broken in Thoroughbred racing these days, in Standardbred racing it happens all the time. The breed continues to improve with each generation, and the original standard of 2 minutes 30 seconds for the mile is now considered very slow. Thirty years ago, a two-minute mile was cause for great excitement; now it's commonplace, and the best Standardbreds have shaved almost 15 seconds off that mark.

Thoroughbred

There's no more finely-tuned racing horse in the world than the Thoroughbred. Bred for over 300 years for speed, the streamlined Thoroughbred is also, in many ways, the ultimate equine athlete, with stamina and jumping ability second to none. But one of the most valuable qualities of the Thoroughbred is one you can't see — an indefinable characteristic called heart, giving him remarkable courage and will to win.

The ancestry of all modern Thoroughbreds can be traced back to one of three desert stallions: the Darley Arabian, the Byerly Turk and the Godolphin Arabian. All three were imported to England between 1690 and 1728, and crossed with the best British racing mares. The result was a fast and elegant racehorse with all the chiseled features, fleetness and intelligence of the Arabian, but with greater size.

Today Thoroughbred racing is a popular sport in nearly every country in the world. As a result, many Thoroughbreds are considered extremely valuable, and some even become heroes. One of the most famous racing Thoroughbreds of this century was a Canadian-bred stallion named Northern Dancer, who won the Kentucky Derby and the Preakness Stakes in 1964 and went on to become one of the most important sires the breed has ever known. One of the Dancer's foals once sold at auction for $10.2 million! Well over a hundred champions trace their lineage back to Northern Dancer.

The Thoroughbred has also competed, to the very highest levels, in dressage and show jumping, and is considered by far the best breed for the tough and demanding sport of three-day-eventing. His speed and agility also make him an ideal polo pony, and his bloodlines have been used to add size, good looks, courage, stamina and athletic ability to many other breeds of horses and ponies. But most people agree the Thoroughbred is not an ideal children's horse. He is often high-strung and sensitive, and requires a very experienced, subtle rider.

Ranging in height from about 15 to 17 hands, Thoroughbreds come in most solid colors, and often have white face and leg markings. They have fine, chiseled faces, large nostrils to help them take in oxygen when they're running at top speed, deep barrels for larger lung and heart capacity, and relatively slender legs (which can make them prone to injury). Their overall look is lean and mean — exactly what a speedster needs.

Fast Fact

One of the 20th century's most famous Thoroughbreds was Secretariat, who won the Triple Crown in 1973, setting five new speed records in his career. The mighty Big Red ran his final race at Woodbine Racetrack in Toronto, winning by six and a half lengths, and then retired to a long stud career. When he died in 1989, he was found to have a heart twice as large as most other horses'.

Welsh Pony

From the hills and valleys of Wales, in the United Kingdom, comes one of the world's most beloved ponies, the Welsh. In fact, the Welsh pony is four ponies in one.

Little bands of Welsh ponies, less than 12 hands high, have run half-wild over the rough Welsh countryside for almost 2000 years, with little interference from people. At some point in the Welsh pony's history, probably several hundred years ago, two Arabian stallions were allowed to roam free with the ponies in the mountains, and the resulting foals and grandfoals showed the Arabian influence, with pretty dished faces and flowing movement, which remain trademarks of the breed.

The future of the Welsh pony was threatened in the 16th century, when King Henry VIII decreed that all horses in the British Isles under 15 hands be destroyed because they were not useful for warfare. Luckily, because they lived in remote, desolate areas where the king's servants were reluctant — or unable — to go, the Welsh ponies were never found, and so they continued to flourish.

Over the years there has been an increasing demand for larger ponies who retain all the best traits of the original Welsh pony. Careful additions of Hackney and Thoroughbred blood eventually resulted in four distinct types of Welsh ponies.

The Welsh Mountain Pony is the original Welsh, standing 12 hands high or less. Another version, called a Section B, is larger, created by cross-breeding Welsh Mountain mares with a small Thoroughbred stallion named Merlin. They stand between 12 and 13:2 hands, and are able to carry larger children, but have kept all the snappy movement and elegance of their smaller cousins. The Welsh Pony of Cob Type also stands up to 13:2 hands, but is heavier and stockier than a Section B. Largest of all is the Welsh Cob, which can actually stand up to 15:2 hands — horse-sized — because of the Andalusian blood in his background. Welsh Cobs are broad-backed and sturdy, can carry an adult with ease, and are known for their endurance and their flashy action at the trot. They were much in demand over Britain's history for use in mounted infantry and for pulling heavy guns and equipment in times of war.

All four types of Welsh ponies are popular worldwide, both as riding and driving ponies. Not only are they charmingly pretty and wonderful jumpers, they are also extremely intelligent and affectionate. Welsh ponies come in most solid colors, although gray, bay, chestnut and buckskin are the most common.

Fast Fact The United Kingdom has more breeds of native ponies than anywhere else in the world — nine, in total. In addition to the Welsh, from Wales, there are the Exmoor, Dartmoor, Fell, Dales and New Forest, all from Britain; the Shetland and Highland ponies from Scotland; and the Connemara from Ireland.

See page 3 for the full-page photo of the Welsh pony.

Saddle Up!

Horse lovers can compete in all kinds of different activities:

Dressage: a form of riding which emphasizes the correct training, and the grace and beauty, of the horse. You are tested by riding a pattern in a rectangular ring, one rider at a time. Movements include circles, diagonal lines and changes of direction at the walk, trot and canter.

Show Hunter: in a hunter show, horses are judged on how smoothly and carefully they clear a series of eight to ten jumps, set up in a pattern. It looks effortless, but it actually takes lots and lots of practice! Riders may also be judged on their riding skills in a hunter equitation class.

Western Pleasure: your horse wears Western tack, and you wear a cowboy hat, leather chaps and cowboy boots. Your horse is judged on how slow and smooth a ride he is, at the walk, jog (a slow trot) and lope. This class is based on the way cowboys would select a pleasurable horse to ride when they had to spend all day in the saddle on the ranch.

Gymkhana or **Western Games:** fast Western action, with many different timed events such as barrel racing, pole bending and the flag race. The fastest horse to complete the pattern wins!

Polo: a fast-paced game of hockey on horseback. Four horses and riders form a team, and the playing field is about three football fields long.

Eventing: an equine triathlon, combining dressage, show jumping and cross-country. Cross-country, the heart of this sport, is the most exciting part: you and your horse gallop through fields and woods, jumping obstacles that are built to look like part of the natural landscape. You may even splash into a water hazard, or jump up a set of horse-sized stairs. You get a combined score based on your performance in all three phases.

Endurance Riding: this sport tests you and your horse's stamina in a trail ride many miles long — from 30 to over 100! You may have to splash through streams, make it across sand dunes or climb a mountain. In competitive trail riding you try to match an optimum time; in endurance racing, the fastest horse wins. Both types of endurance riding monitor the health of the horses extremely closely, allowing only those horses who are fit and sound to continue on the ride.

Pleasure Driving: your horse pulls an elegant carriage; you hold the reins, wearing a traditional driving apron and a hat. You are judged on your horse's obedience and training and on your turn-out (how pleasant and correct a picture you make to the judge).

What's My Color?

Chestnut: a reddish, coppery or orange coat, with the mane, tail, lower legs, muzzle and ear tips the same color as the body. Sometimes the mane and tail are a little lighter than the body — they may even be "flaxen" (cream-colored).

Sorrel: a light chestnut, verging on blond.

Bay: body color is red to brown, and the points are black. A dark bay might be called a "mahogany bay," while a bright red one is a "blood bay."

Liver chestnut: the color of raw liver, with mane and tail the same color.

Black: black all over, including the points. True blacks are rare, so look for a black muzzle. If it's brown, the horse is dark bay or brown, not black.

Brown: just misses being a black by having a brown muzzle; also called dark bay.

Buckskin: a yellow or golden color with black points. Buckskins may also have a dorsal stripe.

Dun: like a buckskin, but usually darker or smokier, ranging from slate gray to yellowish to red.

Grulla (pronounced GREW-ya) a type of dun, in which the base color is a mousy brown-gray (*grulla* is Spanish for mouse). *Grullas* have dorsal stripes and zebra striping on their legs.

Gray: mixed white and dark hairs all over the body. Mane and tail may be the same color as the body, lighter (sometimes pure white) or darker.

Roan: a horse which has white hairs scattered throughout its coat.

Palomino: a golden coat with a white or creamy mane and tail.

Cremello or ***perlino*:** a pale yellow or creamy color with white or cream mane and tail.

Piebald: a Pinto or Paint horse that is black and white.

Skewbald: a Pinto or Paint that is white with any other color except black. For instance, a skewbald may be bay and white, or chestnut and white.

The mystery of how coat colors work is one of the things that keeps breeders trying. With each long-anticipated foal, it's a gamble — you never know what you're going to get!

Fast Fact

Gray horses are born some other color, such as chestnut or bay, and as they mature they "gray out," gradually turning gray and then getting lighter and lighter as they age. An old gray horse may appear to be pure white, but he is still called a gray. The only true "white" horse is an albino, one born without pigment in his coat.

Hot, Cold and Warm

What does it mean when breeders say they want to add a dash of "cold blood" to their breeding program?

Which breeds are the most "hot blooded"? And what, exactly, is a "warmblood"?

Hot, cold and warm are terms used to describe a horse's background and temperament. Only two breeds, the Arabian and the Thoroughbred, are considered to be "hot bloods" — a way of saying they are fiery, sensitive and fast. In contrast, the draft or "heavy horse" breeds, such as the Clydesdale, Shire, Belgian, Percheron and Suffolk Punch, are considered to be "cold bloods" — meaning they are naturally built for power instead of speed, and have quiet and gentle dispositions.

Most of the horse breeds in the world today combine the best qualities of both hot-blooded and cold-blooded horses together. This makes them "warm-blooded" breeds. Any horse which results from a cross of draft-type horses with Arabians or Thoroughbreds can be correctly described as a warmblood. However, in recent years the term "warmblood" has been given a slightly different meaning. Now it is usually used to describe a type of horse bred in European countries for the Olympic sports of dressage, show jumping and three-day-eventing. The German breeds such as the Hanoverian, Trakehner, Oldenburger and Westphalian are all considered warmbloods, as are breeds from other countries, such as the Dutch Warmblood, Swedish Warmblood and the *Selle Français* (from France). Warmblood breeds are becoming very popular around the world, since they have been bred for excellent athletic ability and easygoing temperaments, making them suitable for many types of riders. Because they are so admired, they often have big price tags, and North Americans often make special trips to Europe to see and buy these horses at huge auction sales.

Fast Fact

Many breeds of horses claim the title "most versatile" — but only one competition every year really proves who's the best at lots of sports. That's the TELUS Battle of the Breeds, held at Spruce Meadows in Calgary, Alberta. In 1998 it was spots on top, as Team Appaloosa took home the first-place honors. Now that's versatile!

Fast Fact

Breeding for a certain color isn't simple. Breeding two horses of a special color together doesn't always result in a foal the same color. If you mate two palominos together, for example, you usually get a washed-out version of the color, called a cremello. Or you might get a chestnut foal. The best chance of getting a palomino foal is to mate a palomino parent with a chestnut one.

For more information:

ANDALUSIAN
The International Andalusian and Lusitano
Horse Association
101 Carnoustie North, Box 200
Birmingham, Alabama
35242 USA
http://www.andalusian.com

APPALOOSA
Appaloosa Horse Club of Canada
Box 940
Claresholm, Alberta   T0L 0T0

Appaloosa Horse Club, Inc.
5070 Highway 8 West
Moscow, Idaho
83843 USA
e-mail marketys@appaloosa.com
http://www.appaloosa.com

ARABIAN
Canadian Arabian Horse Registry
#801, 4445 Calgary Trail South
Edmonton, Alberta   T6H 5R7

International Arabian Horse Association
10895 East Bethany Drive
Aurora, Colorado
80014-2605 USA
http://www.iaha.com

CANADIAN
Société des Éleveurs de Chevaux Canadiens
Michel Dostre, secretary/treasurer
349 rang St. Charles
St. Aimé, Quebec   J0G 1K0
http://www.clrc.on.ca/canadian.html

http://www.horses.nl/rassen/canadian.html
http://www.canadianhorses.com/history.html

HANOVERIAN
Hanoverian Breeders Club of Eastern Canada
12 Country Club Drive
Etobicoke, Ontario   M9A 3J4

American Hanoverian Society
4067 Iron Works Parkway
Lexington, Kentucky
40511 USA
http://www.hanoverian.org

ICELANDIC
The United States Icelandic Horse Congress
38 Park St.
Montclair, New Jersey
07042 USA
http://www.icelandics.org

http://www.hestur.com/cihf

MORGAN
Canadian Morgan Horse Association, Inc.
Nancy Kavanaugh, Administrator
Box 286
Port Perry, Ontario   L9L 1E4
http://www.osha.igs.net/+cmha/index.html

American Morgan Horse Association
P.O. Box 960
Shelburne, Vermont
05482-0960 USA
e-mail info@morganhorse.com
http://www.morganhorse.com

PAINT and PINTO
American Paint Horse Association
P.O. Box 961023
Fort Worth, Texas 76161-0023 USA
e-mail askapha@alpha.com
http://www.apha.com

Canadian Pinto Horse Association
Box 729
Bragg Creek, Alberta   T0L 0K0

PASO FINO
The Paso Fino Horse Association
101 North Collins St.
Plant City, Florida
33566-3311 USA

Peruvian Horse Association of Canada
Gus McCollister
Lyalta, Alberta   T0J 1Y0
e-mail phac@netway.ab.ca
http://www.peruvian-pasos.com/phac.html

The Paso Fino Horse Association, Inc.
http://www.pasofino.org

QUARTER HORSE
American Quarter Horse Association
P.O. Box 200
Amarillo, Texas
79168 USA
http://www.aqha.com

America's Quarter Horse
http://www.quarterh.com:8080/

AMERICAN SADDLEBRED
American Saddlebred Horse Association
4093 Iron Works Parkway
Lexington, Kentucky 40511 USA
http://www.asha.net

American Saddlebred Information Source
http://www.trot.org

American Saddlebred Home Page
http://www.saddlebred.agriequine.com/asbasha
.html

American Saddlebred Home Page
http://www.american_saddlebred.com

Saddlebred Page for Kids
http://www.geocities.com/EnchantedForest/Dell/
1330/

SHETLAND PONY
Canadian Pony Society
c/o Debbie Dykstra,
RR #1, Jarvis, Ontario   N0A 1J0

American Miniature Horse Association
5601 South Interstate 35 W.
Alvarado, Texas, 76009 USA
e-mail amha@flash.net
http://www.minihorses.com/amha/

SHIRE
The Canadian Shire Horse Association
Peggy Chapman, Secretary
1297 Eldon Road, RR #1
Oakwood, Ontario   K0M 2M0

The American Shire Horse Association
http://www.shirehorse.org

OTHER DRAFT BREEDS
Clydesdale Breeders of the USA
17346 Kelley Road
Pecatonica, Illinois 61603 USA
http://members.aol.com/clydesusa/

Belgian Draft Horse Corp. of America
P.O. Box 335
Wabask, Indiana
46992 USA

Percheron Horse Assoc. of America
P.O. Box 141
10330 Quaker Road
Fredericktown, Ohio   43019 USA
http://www.percheronhorse.org

STANDARDBRED
Standardbred Canada
2150 Meadowvale Blvd.
Mississauga, Ontario   L5N 6R6
http://www.trotcanada.ca

United States Trotting Association
750 Michigan Avenue
Columbus, Ohio 43215-1191 USA
http://www.ustrotting.com

THOROUGHBRED
The Canadian Thoroughbred Horse Societ
(National Division)
P.O. Box 172
Rexdale, Ontario   M9W 5L1

The Jockey Club
821 Corporate Drive
Lexington, Kentucky
40503-2794 USA
http://www.jockeyclub.com

http://www.imh.org/imh/bw/tbred.html

WELSH PONY
Welsh Pony and Cob Society of America
P.O. Box 2977
Winchester, Virginia
22604-2977 USA

**NOTE: addresses and website
information are accurate at the
time of publication.**